DEDIC

This publication is dedicated to my late son *Thor Nigel Williams (13/8/71 –19/7/95).*

Thor was a disciple of the *dancehall* and in fact he cut several records under the name *Daddy Tar.* Of the lot, one, *Zigzawya,* did quite well and became number one on the *Black British Charts* for several weeks.

He however enjoyed his job as an *Entertainment Coordinator* at the Couples, Tower Isle, as that offered him unlimited opportunities to perform on stage with both resident and visiting bands.

It was his enthusiasm for the *dancehall* which exposed me to the emerging language (*the new street lingo*) and inspired my research which led to the birth of the *first edition of "Original Dancehall Dictionary"* in *1993.*

At the time of his untimely death, we were working on the *Second Edition* and I know he is happy that this publication *has become a bestseller* and that I have continued to upgrade it.

Thanks Thor. Your spirit lives on in many ways and definitely in this publication.

FOREWORD AND ACKNOWLEDGEMENT

This is the *sixth Edition* of the **ORIGINAL DANCEHALL DICTIONARY** and by far the most comprehensive.

I can't recall having more fun researching and writing a book, for the laughs were endless. This is because the **street lingo** is evolving daily and is being immediately reinforced in the *dancehalls* island-wide.

True, a number of the words and phrases are the same or similar to *old time patois*, but many have been modified by the youth to mean *the very opposite* of what they originally did. No matter how you look at it however, this street language being developed by the youth is extremely expressive, catchy and in the main, hilarious.

To do this upgrade however, I could never have reached anywhere without the exuberant assistance of my knowledgeable young friends who keep me up to date with every beat on the streets and in the **dancehalls.** Let me therefore express my heartfelt gratitude to these worthy teachers who unfortunately do not want their names published.

And of course a million thanks to my brilliant illustrator *Shawn Grant* whose cartoons have added so much life to the publications.

ALL RIGHTS RESERVED

ORIGINAL DANCEHALL DICTIONARY

SIXTH EDITION

A Bills: A Jamaican $100 bill. This can no longer pay for the simplest task and many a beggar will look at it scornfully and tell you in no uncertain terms that *"dis caan buy nutten"!*

A Boom: A general term meaning...*good things are happening.... one's luck is changing for the better, life is great* etc.

A Deh So It Deh: *It's a fact, that's how it is* or *that's the way the way the cookie crumbles!*

A Deh So Di Current Deh; *That's where I get my information.*

A Di Lik: *That's the latest style.*

A Im Run Tings: *He is the boss...the Don.*

A It (hit) Mi A Defen: A very dogmatic way of saying *that one supports or is in*

favour of something.
However when it's preceded by the phrase *"right now"* it becomes very clear that that one is only lending *temporary support.*

A Manley: A Jamaican $1,000 note. *Very few things cost any less these days*.

A Nuh Nutten: *Think nothing of it,* or *that's not important.*

A Nuh Pram Push Ting: *"It is not as easy* (to accomplish) *as it appears."* A *pram* is a baby's carriage. **See the logic?**

A Step-up Time: *A step up time* but mi haffi beat some juice fus." **Translation.** Although it is time for me to go out and earn some money, I must have something to drink first. *Step up time* is most often used in the context of setting out to acquire funds *by fair or foul means.* However it is sometimes used to suggest that it is *time to get going or leave the scene.* It has now gained some respectability in

4

certain circles meaning ***time to set out to improve one's status in life.***

A Suh Di Ting Set Up: *That's life*....usually used when another party is complaining about

A Wah Dis Fada: *An expression of disbelief.* For example, a pedestrian is splashed by a speeding motorists. He views the action of the driver with utmost disbelief and exclaims. ***"But a wah dis fada!"***

A Wah Im Deh Pan: *What's his her problem? Why is he /she acting like that?*

A Wah Yu A Defen? *What do you have to say for yourself? What is your opinion? Exactly what do you believe in?* One has to decipher the exact meaning depending on the context in which the expression is used.

A Wan: *Someone* or *somebody*. **Example**. *A wan tief mi money outta mi packet.* **Translation**.

Someone stole my money out of my pocket. Interestingly however, when we say *wi a wan*, it does not mean *we are somebody (of renown)*, but rather *we are brothers* or *we are united.* (In other words "we are one" people)

Accident: *Dat dey gala accident fi true !*
Translation That young lady is so ugly that she obviously was an unplanned pregnancy! ie. *An accident.*
Dance Hall lyrics *tend to be rather sexist* and sometimes quite cruel.
Accident is a word used to describe an *ugly woman*. We wait with bated breath to hear what the *male equivalent is*.

All Gravy Man: This simply means *Everything is fine* or *all is well.*

Alms House: As you know, an *alms house* is supposed to be a refuge for poor people. In most instances however, conditions there are terrible. So in the *dancehall* context the term has evolved to describe any action or sentiment that *is disgusting, disgraceful or degrading.*

Example: *Imagine sey a ole man lakka Benjie a try fi check di likkle school   pickney gal dem. Dat a alms house bisiness, yu nuh seet* .
Translation. Imagine an old man like Benjie is going around trying to seduce school girls. That is so disgraceful. He should be ashamed of himself.

An Ting: And so on and so forth.

Anaconda: *A very large penis...every Jamaican man's dream.* This new word was a well kept secret for quite a while until it led to great controversy and a legal battle. This happened because a local songwriter wrote a song for a *Japanese female* performer but failed to explain the meaning of *Anaconda* to her. When she performed the song to those who knew the true meaning, she was seriously embarrassed, hence the lawsuit. Only then did *anaconda* came out of the proverbial closet.

Angle: *To treat one with disrespect.* The origin of this word is however **handle,** *but who the heck bothers with the letter "H" these days?* **Example;** *Dem angle di bway bad yu si.*

Translation I was so sorry for the young man as they treated him like a dog.

Ankle Express: *To travel by foot*.....and in light of the numerous luxurious vehicles that grace our shores, there is now a bit of prejudice against those who are unable to drive a car. So when one refers to a person traveling by *ankle express,* it tends to be said with a hint of snobbery. **Example**....*yu si how Monica gwaan like shi stoosh? Well a ankle express shi haffi tek go work yu know"*. **Translation**. Despite the fact that Monica acts like she is a person of great wealth and class, she cannot even afford to buy a car and has to walk to work.

Artical: *(Sometimes "Hortical or Hartical")* Regardless of how it is spelt or pronounced, this is one of those words with multiple meanings. Originally, it meant *militant.* Then it evolved to convey the idea that one is the best in a particular field. **Eg.** The *Artical Don* is the most vicious gunman within the group or **the area leader.**

Anyway, **Artical** has again evolved to *mean **a person who is cool, easy to deal with** or even **a good friend**.*
Example. *Im artical man.*
Translation. He is such a nice person.

A Suh Di Ting Set Up: *That is how it is* (or going to be) *so you had better learn to live with it!*

Babylon: Originally, the police were called **Babylon.** However the word evolved to refer to anything evil or bad. So **bun fire pon babylon** has become a regular phrase **in dancehall** lingo.

Back an Belly Rat: Yu caan trus dem dey bwoy far dem a **back an belly rat.** Those people cannot be trusted because they are hypocrites. Beware for this type of **rat** is a backstabber, hypocrite or spy, *but then aren't all rats like that?* (Without even the back and belly embellishment?)

Bad Cansequencies: *There will be terrible repercussions.* (This phrase is usually used as a threat).

Bagga Mout: *Empty words or false promises.* Politicians are notorious for their **bagga mout!**

Bandoolo: *Anything illegal.* **Yard** is the home

of *Anancy*, and since according to one influential government minister *those who play by the rules get shafted*, almost everything **has to be done** *Bandoolo style....bandoolo passports, bandoolo birth certificates, bandoolo US visas, bandoolo name brand clothes...*you name it and we got it *bandoolo style.* The noun is *bandoolism.*

Bashey: *Anything that looks good, whether human or matter.* So a man or woman can be described as *bashey.* As can a fabulous outfit, a nice car or whatever. You choose, as long as it's really *bashey!*

Bashment: This was originally *a party or dance* or any other *social gathering* where modern *Yard* music (read *dancehall* music) was played. However *bashment* has now become a general **adjective** to describe *anything that is top of the line or very desirable.*

Bashment Bus: Here, *bashment* is not an adjective as described above, but rather it is noun, part of a name given to minibuses *that are driven very fast*

with loud lewd music
blaring and where all behaviour is
" acceptabl"e behaviour. The
bashement bus is a favourite among
most teenage "*schoolers.*"

Bashment Ride: *What wild young schoolgirls
usually get* (or hope to get) on a
bashment bus.

Batta Batta: This is a *verb* meaning *to hang
around or to pass one's time
aimlessly.* **Example.** *Mi si di bwaay a
batta batta roun di place.*
Translation. I saw the young man
hanging around outside. The young
man in this case would be the **"batta
foot." (Noun.)**

Batta Bout: *Some a di man dem luv wen di **batta bout**
gal dem cum a dance yu si an dem even
ride dem bare back.* **Translation**: Some
men love to see the loose women at
dancehall sessions. And despite the
prevalence of **AIDS**, many will have sex
without giving a second thought to
using any form of protection. ***Batta
bout*** is usually used to describe *only
women,* for in **dancehall** *parlance*

there is no such thing as a *loose man*.

Batta Foot: In years gone by one would have heard something like, "*But a ow dat dey batta foot bwaay did expec fi go inna di session?*" **Translation:** Did that barefooted man really expect that he would have been allowed to enter the club dressed as he is? *Batta foot* was then the term used for people who were too poor to wear shoes (as opposed to those who walk barefooted as a matter of preference).Today, *batta foot is* generally used to describe *people who go around aimlessly or people who wander around making a pest of themselves because they have nothing better to do.*

Batty Rider: A pair of *panties disguised as shorts.* The only difference being that the *batty rider* is generally made from sturdier material than *the lowly drawers.*

Beat Some Juice: "Di sun so hat dat if mi nuh *beat some juice* mi a go ded." **Translation.** It is so hot outside today that if I do not get

a cold drink soon, I will be
totally dehydrated. Simply put,
beat some juice means *to have a drink*

Beat Some Bine or **Blow Bine:** Fram di
friction start between Bugsy
and Smilie wi cyaan sleep a
nite far dem jus a ***blow
bine*** non stop.n **Translation.** Ever
since Bugsy and Smilie quarreled we
have been unable to sleep at
nights as they are constantly shooting
as each other. Both terms *mean firing
shots or shooting.*

Ben Up: *Seething with anger.*

Big Up: "Wi haffi go a di dance tinite *fi big up*
Likkle Yout." **Translation**. As our friend
Little Youth will be performing tonight
we have to be there to applaud him. *Big
Up* means *to salute, applaud or praise
someone.*

Bimmer: *A BMW motor car*. This term is now
being used internationally. Anyway, in
the **dancehall**, the BMW is considered
one of the ultimate "***Bling Blings.***" It is
therefore not surprising that a special
word for this vehicle crept into

dancehall lingo.

Blab: *A fat or grossly overweight person.* Eg. Dat dey
   blab nuh know sey a ongle mawga people
   fi wear dem dey style clothes. **Translation.**
   Doesn't that fat man look awful in that outfit?

Bless Up: *Goodbye, see you later.* (Also,as below)

Blessed or Bless: An uplifting salutation meaning
   Greetings, Selassie be with you,
   walk good etc. or simply, *see you*
   later.

Bligh or Bly: *A break, an advantage, an*
   opportunity or special treatment.

Bling Out: *Looking fabulous and prosperous.*
   Example. "What a way Kim ***bling out***.
   Har man mussi jus sen out a shipment."
   Translation. Look at Kim's brand name
   clothes and jewellery and the
   fabulous car that she is driving. Her
   boyfriend must have succeeded in sending
   out a shipment of drugs for her to be able
   to afford such expensive
   trappings.

Bling Bling: *The trappings of wealth, beauty and fine*
   style....the things that allow people to

Bling Out, *material things that is.* This has led *snob society* to speak disparagingly about the *Bling Bling mentality*. In other words, the worshipping of material possessions by those *who have just arrived* or who are *waiting to arrive.* Anyway, since **Yardies** are the greatest at inventing everything including language, **bling bling** has now been incorporated into the leading dictionaries of the world, namely **Webster's and Oxford. Original Dancehall Dictionary,** take a bow for having *first recorded* this term in the annals of **great dictionaries**!

Blood A Go Run: A threat of violent confrontation. **Example**. *Di big man bring in some new M16 so mi no sey blood a go run tinite.* **Translation.** We had better be careful tonight as the gunmen have been rearmed and we know they will be going on a killing spree.

Bob Marley: This is the name given to *a large spliff.* **Bob Marley's** most famous poster is the one of him with a large lighted spliff in his mouth, hence the name. So if you go up to your local supplier on the sidewalk, you need to be specific. For if you simply say, *gimmi a spliff nuh spar,* you could end up with a *Ziggy...* a cigarette size ganja spliff.

Bodyguard: This means the same as *Joe Grine...the man on the side...the one who entertains the lady when the cat's away.* When a *bodyguard* is hovering around, the result is usually *a jacket!*

Bokkle Boom: *A molotov cocktail...a primitive bomb.*

Bomb Rush: What happens when a number of top class **DJ's** are on stage and much to the delight of the audience, they take turns at grabbing the microphone in an effort to outdo each other. In short, *on stage competition among DJ's.*

Bomshell: *A loose woman.*

Bonafied: *Real, genuine or true.* **Example.** "Rocky a *mi bonafied bredren yu know*".**Translation**. Rocky has been a real f riend to me over the years. *Bonafied* can be used to refer *to persons or things.*

Boom Head: *A gullible girl, one who is easily*

17

controlled. In the ***olden days*** this same girl would be described as ***empty headed*** or if white, a ***dumb blond.*** (However, since a number of persons of every colour who go to **dancehall** sessions these days are false blonds, *dumb blond* would not work here!) Another term used instead of ***boom head*** is ***Pan Handle.***

Boops: *"Si di boops dey, wi haffi nyam im out."* That's a line from the famous song that popularized the word. *A boops is a man (*usually an older man*) who opens up himself to financial exploitation by women.*

Boopsie: "Shi caan bruk far shi a ***boopsie*** and di man hab nuff money" **Translation.** She is never broke as she has a very rich man catering *to* her every need. The ***boopsie is a woman who preys on the Boops*** and sometimes she even has several ***"Boopses"*** at a time. One pays the rent, another buys the car, one supplies the top of the line cell phones etc. etc.

Bounce Check : *A false promise. Insincerity.* **Example.** Bway, Juanita promise mi a date but mi jus

18

know a **bounce check** dat .
Translation. Jauanita promised to go out with
me but I am not setting my mind on it
as I suspect she was only toying
with my emotions.

Bow: One of the many words used in the **dancehall** for
oral sex. (Most male performers at these
hallowed halls claim not to indulge in this
wonderful act, however their girlfriends often
say it's a different matter when they get under
the sheets!) **Example:** *Rastaman nuh bow, yu
nuh seet.* **Translation.** *Oral sex is a no no to
us clean living Rastafarians.* However, **bow**
has a less spectacular meaning...that is *giving
in or submitting to another.* **Example:** *Mi
nuh bow to no man.* **Translation.** *No one can
order me around.* It is therefore imperative
that you listen carefully to the context in which
bow is being used *in order to avoid serious
embarrassment!!!!*

Bow Cat: A man *who relishes oral sex.*

Box Cover: *Back a Yard* we are known for our
colourful expressions, many of which
can attract a fine in the courts, if
you happen to use them in the presence
of a policeman. Among our most

colourful expressions are a number which begin with **B.C.** Whenever a child wishes to use one of these colourful expressions but an adult is around or when a timid adult wishes to do the same but a policeman is within earshot, the relatively innocuous expression **Box Cover** can save one the penalties while allowing the user to let off steam. Basically therefore, *box cover* is just a harmless *expression of surprise or amazement.*

Bredren: "Mi always look out fi mi *bredren* dem know" **Translation**. I always protect my friends' interests. *Your bredren is your friend.......someone closer than a brother.* The word is also often used **as a pleasant greeting** and recently there has been a trend in certain areas to use *"Breds"* instead of *"Bredren."*

Brinks: This is another word used to describe men *who allow themselves to be financially* exploited by women. *Men with deep pockets.* The same as *Boops.*

Broutupsy: *Manners, good breeding. Eg.* Yu nuh ha nuh *broutupsy* bwaay. **Translation**

21

You are an ill mannered creature.

Browning: *A person of fair complexion,* usually used as a compliment. So if you are fair, do not be offended if someone shouts *"Hey browning."* For according to **dancehall** culture *it is a great thing to be.* In fact, such a greeting usually carries a tone of admiration attached to it and some would give their bottom dollar to be addressed as such. This has led to an epidemic of *skin bleaching*, and interestingly, *even men are doing it.* Check out *Vybes Kartel, he is now a browning!*

Bruk Out: This simple expression can mean many things to different people. It can mean quite generally to *have fun.* At times it is an expression used by men in the **dancehall** to encourage their mates *to show off* or *make their presence felt on the dance floor.* On the other hand, some teenage girls who have lived under strict parental control, use *bruk out* when boasting that *they have finally had the sexual experience.*

Bruk Paket Bway: *A man who has no money to*

22

wine and dine (or otherwise support) a lady. This phrase is generally used to *insult men* who are trying to make dates outside of their accepted circle. However it can be a *general insult* thrown at any man *who deserves a cursing!*

Bubble: *To be up to date on the latest dance moves and perform them with much vigor and vitality.* Women with fantastic bodies who know how to gyrate and get the crowd moving are often referred to as **bubblers.**

Buffilous: "Yu did know sey Joan a waan *buffilous* dawta?" **Translation:** Did you know that Joan has a very sexy body? **Buffilous** is one of the many words used in the dancehall to describe *the beauty of a well rounded female body.*

Bumper: A *lady's bottom....that part of our lovely structure which was created solely for the delight of the Jamaican male.* (**That is if one was to draw conclusions from the unsolicited comments of our dear brazen men folk!**)

Bumper Rider: A garment *resembling a panty* which

23

exposes a woman's *bumper.* Kith and kin of a *Batty Rider.*

Bun Bun: *A cookery term. This is food which is slightly burnt, a great delicacy to some* **Yar***dies.* **Eg.** Mi luv di *bun bun* part a di meat. **Translation.** My meat has to be slightly burnt for me to enjoy it.

Bun: The standard *bun*, is a favourite pastry with us a *Yard,* especially at **Easter** time. However, the popular "**bun**" means *to commit adultery, be unfaithful...gi yu partna bun.* In the **dancehall** however, **bun** is also used *to heap condemnation on the heads of certain types of people or lifestyles.* **Example.** *Bun dung Babylon* or *bun all hypocrite.* **Translation.** Down with the powers that be or away with all hypocrites.

Bun Im: *Hurt Him (*by sleeping with another man*)*! This is advice freely given to women who are having problems with their partners. It means *be unfaithful to him.* The famous female DJ **Makka Diamond** made a monster hit giving women advice on this matter. So if the man is being unfaithful to his special woman, the chorus from her friends would be, "**bun fi bun**". *Translation.* Since he is having an

25

affair, you also need to have one!

Bun Head (Ead): *People who use chemicals or hot combs to straighten their hair are said to have **bun ead.** (h)* This is no longer an insult but reality all around!

Bun A Man Kin: "Mi nuh kin up *fi **bun a man kin,*** yu nuh seet. **Translation.** I have no compunction about torturing or killing people who offend me, do you understand? ***Bun a man kin*** *means doing physical harm to someone.*

Bun Bad Candle: *Work obeah.*

Bun Calory: *Have sex.* **(sexercise)**

Bun Tiya: "***Bun tiya*** driber, yu nuh si di bwaay a ketch yu up. **Translation.** Step on the gas driver, can't you see that the other bus is hot on your tail. ***Bun tiya*** is *an order to drive fast or step on the gas,* a frequent command given by passengers to drivers *of public buses and taxis....* hence the high rate of accidents among those vehicles.

Bus Out: *What happens when a D.J becomes famous.* **Example.** Yu memba ow Pack a Mout use fi travel pan *ten toe turbo?* Well since im bus out a pure Bimmer im dribe an pure cargo im a moggle yu know."
Translation: Do you remember the days when Pack A Mouth used to walk barefooted? Well since he became a famous **DJ,** he drives a spanking new BMW and wears a lot of gold jewellery.

Bus Shat: "Di bwaay dem run yu si, wen di Dads come out *an bus shat* afta dem.
Translation. The young men escaped quickly when the Don arrived on the scene and started to fire his gun at them. *Bus shat* is another of the numerous phrases developed in the dancehall to describe the use of a gun. In fact it is very popular for some fans to even bus shat at stage shows to demonstrate their approval of outstanding performances and those who have no guns or are not inclined to use them, use their fingers to indicate that they are firing weapons. Our version *of a 21 gun salute* I guess!

Bush Telegram*: Rumour*. How messages are informally transmitted.

Caan Tess: *Dear not challenge. Challenging me would be a waste of your energy.* In other words, *I am the greatest!*

Calleck Shell: *A threat to shoot someone.* The person is invited to collect shells *ie. gunshots.*

Cannibal: *Someone who indulges in **oral sex.*** Oral sex is often criticized in **dancehall** lyrics although many of those who protest the loudest *are often the most avid practitioners themselves! (*under the cover of darkness naturally.)

Cargo Dung: *Ostentatiously decked out in lots of (*large gold*) jewellery.* This is the ultimate manifestation of wealth and success in the **Dancehall.** (A Hummer, Bimmer, Escalade or F350 parked outside does no harm either!)

Catty: Another of the many words used in the **dancehall** *to describe a woman.* In my opinion, this is a step up from *"Beef"* however.

Chalwa: Another word for a *chalice*...the pipe in which our *"weed of wisdom"* is smoked.

Chat Bout: *I agree with you* or *I like what you are saying*.

Champion Bubbla: *A woman* (usually one with a voluptuous figure) *who is versed in the latest dances on the* **dancehall** *circuit and who performs on the dance floor with much vigour*. You must be a *champion bubbla* to enter the annual *dancehall queen* competition.

Check Fi: *Liking someone in romantic* or *lustful way*. **Example**. Mi *check fi* da dawta deh far shi well *buffilous*. **Translation**. I am in love with that young lady as she is the most voluptuous creature I have ever seen. Alternatively, it used to mean *like or admire*. **Example**. Mi *check fi* da yout yu know far im well conscious. **Translation**. I would help out that young man anytime because I really admire his zeal. One therefore has to listen carefully to the context in which the phrase is used.

Chemical Duppy: Originally, this was used in reference to a man who uses *Jerry Curl* in his hair. It has however been more widely adopted to describe any black person who uses chemicals to disguise the texture of his or her hair and bleaches the face. Another term also used for persons involved in such activity was *Chemical Coolie.* The stigma that was attached to these activities however, no longer exists as anything that can bring one close to becoming a *Browning* is usually welcomed by hard core *dancehall* fans. In fact, based on the pictures one sees coming from most **dancehall** sessions, one could conclude that **Jamaica** now has very few really *black people.*

Chill Out: *Relax, enjoy one's self, pass the time in a pleasant manner.* At times one simply says to another *chill nuh man*. This is an order for the offending party to *calm down*.

Chi Chi Man: In the olden days, a *chi chi* was a termite... an insect which is greatly

feared as many persons had been known to lose their homes after a visit by termites. Then for some strange reason *chi chi* was adopted as the name of the publicly owned bus that served the Kingston area. Then suddenly *chi chi* became another name for a *male homosexual.* This term was popularised by a *dancehall* group which immediately shot to fame when they made a tune bashing homosexuals who they described *chi chi man.* This song also created quite a political storm as immediately one of the leading political parties a *Yard* started to brand the leader of the other leading party a *chi chi* man. After that, the popular tune could never played in the precincts of meetings held by the party whose leader had been defamed. Next, *chi chi man* started to have international implications as powerful *gay lobby group*s took exception to the various calls from **Jamaican DJ's** to harm those so sexually oriented. In fact, the lobby was so powerful that many **DJ's** have been prevented from performing at some stage shows abroad. Now that they are feeling it in their pockets, there is much less use of the term in the **dancehalls.** Anyway, at first I did not understand how the inoffensive term *chi chi* could have evolved to mean **a gay man**. Then a reader explained it to me. He said that since originally *chi chi* was an insect which **ate wood**. It was a natural progression for an insect (read man) which **eats hood** to be called a *chi chi man? (*So a get it so a gi it, mi nuh mek nuh profit)

Chuck Badness: *Intimidate others* (using threats of physical violence.) A more moderate term is *Chuck It* meaning *verbally insulting someone.*

Claffy: *An imbecile or simpleton.*

Clean Steel: Another of the many terms used to describe *the firing of or using a gun.*

Colt Di Game: *To disrupt, do something out of the ordinary or disturb the natural order of things.*

Cool Breeze: An all encompassing expression

meaning ***All is well, I understand,
Goodbye***, whatever.

Conshus: *To be creative, positive, uplifting.*
  Example. Bwaay, I an I jus luv cum a
  session wen Gregory dey pan stage far a
  pure *conshus* lyrics im a gi wi.
  Translation. I love to hear Gregory
  perform for his lyrics are always uplifting.

Crew: *Massive, group of pals who do things together.*

Cridell: An *unfaithful woman.* While we tend to coin
  special words and phrases and condemn
  women with more than one mate, men who do
  the same are generally looked upon as role
  models!

Criss: *Nicely or expensively dressed, chic, well put
  together.* However ***eberyting criss*** means all is
  well.

Crissas: *An expensive brand name car.* **Example.**
  Since Bongoman *bus out* a pure *crissas*
  imma drive. **Translation.** Ever since
  Bongoman became a star, he has been
  driving very flashy cars.

Cushu Peng: In the olden days when slackness
  prevailed, *cushu* was a *lady's vagina.*

(Do you remember the mento tune *"pennyreel o"* which said in part...*tun yu cushu gimmi mek mi rub out mi money?*) Well now that our artists are *more respectful* (lol) of women, **cushu peng** has absolutely no slack suggestions but it simply means a *ganja cigarette, a spliff of whatever size.* So when you hear someone say, **mi a go fi mi cushu peng**, please do not allow your dirty mind to wander.

Cyaan Dun: *The epitome of male virility.* In other words, or rather in the words of the boaster, **invincible in bed (and that is without the use of Viagra!)** This is usually only in the mind of the speaker however. In fact, if **Yardie** men were to be believed, everyone of them would have the label *"cyaan dun"* painted on his forehead as that is a kind of national mantra among them.

Cyaan Tess: This *is the mother of all boasts.* If **Mohammed Ali** was speaking, he would say *"I am the greatest"*. But a **Yard** we say *cyaan tess*. In other words, do not *even think of challenging me* (at anything!)

Dads: Originally this was the term used for *a wealthy and influential man in the inner city.....a person who gained his wealth and influence by criminal means.* However the term is used very loosely these days by youths hailing up *big men* who they consider their seniors or someone who they think is in a position to help them financially. Women are called *mumsy* or *mummy.*

Dallaz Man: An *informal foreign exchange trader.*

Dapper: *A man noted for his sexual prowess.* Sometimes it is used to describe an *area leader* or a well respected person. Of course the old time meaning is a *well groomed ma*n.

Dat A Di Lik: *That's how things are done.*

Dawg Hart:Yu si da man deh? Imma *dawg hart* yu know, far im nuh skin up fi *bun man kin,* eff a man eben tep pan im toe."
Translation: Do you see that man over there? Be very careful of him as he is an extremely dangerous person. In fact he is so dangerous that he is reputed to have killed a man who accidentally

from performing at some stage shows abroad. Now that they are feeling it in their pockets, there is much less use of the term in the **dancehalls.** Anyway, at first I did not understand how the inoffensive term *chi chi* could have evolved to mean **a gay man**. Then a reader explained it to me. He said that since originally *chi chi* was an insect which **ate wood**. It was a natural progression for an insect (read man) which **eats hood** to be called a *chi chi man?* (So a get it so a gi it, mi nuh mek nuh profit)

Chuck Badness: *Intimidate others* (using threats of physical violence.) A more moderate term is *Chuck It* meaning *verbally insulting someone.*

Claffy: *An imbecile or simpleton.*

Clean Steel: Another of the many terms used to describe *the firing of or using a gun.*

Colt Di Game: *To disrupt, do something out of the ordinary* or *disturb the natural order of things.*

Cool Breeze: An all encompassing expression

meaning *All is well, I understand, Goodbye*, whatever.

Conshus: *To be creative, positive, uplifting.*
Example. Bwaay, I an I jus luv cum a session wen Gregory dey pan stage far a pure *conshus* lyrics im a gi wi.
Translation. I love to hear Gregory perform for his lyrics are always uplifting.

Crew: *Massive, group of pals who do things together.*

Cridell: An *unfaithful woman.* While we tend to coin special words and phrases and condemn women with more than one mate, men who do the same are generally looked upon as role models!

Criss: *Nicely or expensively dressed, chic, well put together.* However *eberyting criss* means all is well.

Crissas: *An expensive brand name car.* **Example.** Since Bongoman *bus out* a pure *crissas* imma drive. **Translation.** Ever since *Bongoman* became a star, he has been driving very flashy cars.

Cushu Peng: In the olden days when slackness prevailed, *cushu* was a *lady's vagina.*

Deh Pan A Likkle Ends: *Gone on a **runnings.***
Out trying to get some
money *any way, anywhere.*

Dem Time Deh: *See you later.*

Dem Deh Tings Haffi Gwaan: *That's the
natural order of
things, life' like
that etc.*

Dem Nah Ramp: *They are dead serious. They are
not joking.* There is usually an
ominous ring to this statement...
a warning of pending doom.

Deportee: A *deportee* will always be a Y*ardie* who
has **tried a ting** overseas but was caught
and forcefully repatriated to his homeland.
However there is another more interesting
meaning. This word also applies to
reconditioned Japanese cars which have
been imported into **Jamaica.** The
reasoning I guess is that the cars are no
longer useful to the Japanese, so they are
deported to us.

Depressor: An oppressor. The logic is that if one
was truly indeed an oppressor (up), he
would be helping you **up not down.**

39

Webster and all other dictionaries
please note this important point!

Deputy: "Shi a mi deputy so mi haffi look afta har"
Translation. She is my girlfriend so I have to
take care of her. The *deputy* is the woman on
the side, (*as opposed to a one night stand*)
the assistant to the wife.

Di Bigga Baas: *The Don of Dons.* Or sometimes
simply *the one in charge.* (In any
enterprise).

Di Owna Fi Di Yard: (As above) *The real boss. The
person in charge.* **Example.**
Fram *di owna fi di yard* come
back fram farin, Bobsy gaan
and wi caan fine im.
Translation. Since the
Don returned, Bobsy has
made a rapid exit from the
area.

Di Runnings: *The natural order of things, how
things are done, what is to be
expected* etc.

Diamond Sword: *A back stabber or hypocrite.
One who cannot be trusted.*

Dibby Dibby: *A useless, ineffectual, unexciting person. Someone who would be referred to as saaf in the old days.* **Example.** Bobby nuh look bad but im too *dibby dibby.* **Translation.** You know Bobby is not a bad looking fellow but he is such a bore.

Diddle Daddle: This is the **Yard** version of *dilly dally.* Of course this *means to dawdle or waste time.*

Dig Up Mi Ians: *Go for my guns....take them out of hiding.* A threat to shoot someone. This can no longer be regarded as an idle threat as so many people now have guns or access to them.

Dip (N): Another word for a *Deportee.* (defined overleaf). However when used as a **verb** it means *go for one's guns.* (ie. Dip into one's proverbial holster).

Dis: *Disrespect someone.* **Example.** Yu si if a man dis di *Don dadda?* Im affi *splurt* yu know an don't eben tink bout cum back. **Translation:** Anyone who disrespects the *Big Man* has to immediately leave the community, never to return. ***Dissing*** someone is often considered an unforgivable crime.

Dis Any Bway Any Time: The words of a ***braggart*** implying that the speaker thinks he is the ***baddest*** man in town and can treat anyone in the most disrespectful manner and get away with it!

Dis Di Program: *Be uncooperative*. It is more often than not, dangerous *to dis di program* established by a don.

Do Suppen Fi Mi Nuh: *Can you assist me please?* This is the new version of *"beg yu suppen nuh"*.

Don: Strictly speaking, a Don is *a feared gunman* one who controls a loyal cadre of minions (a*ka lesser gunmen.)* However the word is much more loosely used these days to refer to *anyone who is outstanding in a particular field*. So you may hear someone referring to a leading banker as the *Don of the banking sector*. However, this certainly does not mean he employs weapons to achieve this status! Or someone may very well *call you Don or Dads*,

42

because he hopes to get of you good side in order to beg money or ask a special favour.

Don Dadda or **Don Gorgon**: These two terms are interchangeable meaning *the man with the greatest firepower in the area.* Since firepower brings influence, it therefore follows that the person with the greatest firepower controls the territory in question. His minions are the *lesser Dons.*

Downpressa: *One who takes advantage of others.* (oppresses his fellow human beings *by keeping them down.* The logic is that if he were indeed an **oppressor,** he would be helping **others up** in life instead of **keeping them down.** *Downpressa* is the *ital version* of o**ppressor.**

Drap Out: *Die, expire, move on to another life.*

Draw Cyard: "Nuff good DJ who bus out lang time bruk now yu know, far di producer dem *draw cyard* pan dem". **Translation**: There are many good **DJ's** who never earned a cent although their tunes made it to the top of the charts. This is because they have been cheated by their producers.

Draw cyard means *to cheat or fool up people*. In the olden days, the phrase was *Carry Dung* but *Dancehall* has added much finesse to the local parlance!

Ducta: *The person who collects the money on a bus.*

Duh*: An expression of disbelief.* It is the response when a stupid remark is made, like someone expressing the obvious or trying to make a big deal out of nothing.

Dun Wife: *The number one (*favourite*) wife or girlfriend.* The opposite of *"Deputy"*.

Dus or Dus Out: Another of the many terms that mean *to kill someone.*

Eat A Food Offa: Si di Dads dey, mi a go *eat a food offa im.* **Translation.** The big boss has arrived and I have to get some money from him today. *Eat a food offa* someone *is to get money from them without working for it*....this is a more dignified way of expressing one's intention to go begging for money.

Eediat Ting: *Absolute nonsense.* **Example.** A wey dem bwaay a go wid dem dey *eediat ting?* Dem tink wi a fool.**Translation**. Do those people really think that they can impress us with such stupid arguments? They obviously have no respect for our intelligence. However, the word **eediat** by itself cannot be taken simply as it is one of the most *important adjectives* in the vocabulary a **Yard.** For anything that *does not work properly* becomes an instant *eediat ting.* So if the Air Jamaica plane arrives late, it becomes an *eediat plane.* And if the car fails to start it becomes an *eediat car.* Get the drift?

45

Emmanuel A Dweet: "*With God all things are possible.*" This is the *ital* version of that popular phrase.

Everything is Everything:(Ebriting is Ebriting:) *All is well. The good times are here again.*

Evva Reddy*: A sexually prolific man ...a man who is always ready, willing and able to make any woman happy.* (What would they do without *Viagra, Cialis* or the numerous *front en liftas* available on the local market?) *Evva Reddies* (that is the plural please) are of course looked upon with great awe. On the other hand, when the term is used to describe a woman, she is considered *just short of being a prostitute.*

Fada Yout: A Friendly greeting. For example, *hail my brother.*

Farin: Where every *Yardie* wants to go…..apart from the very few who want *to die* and go to heaven! It's not that *Yardies* are not religious people for most want to go to heaven. The point is however, that very few *want to die* in order to go there. Those who think that there is a heaven where one does not have to die to migrate to, *think that heaven is in Farin.* These people are called *farin minded* by those of us who have no wish to migrate (again). Now while *Farin* is technically any country outside of *Yard's* shores….a place that you fly to, when a *Yardie* speaks of going to *Farin,* he *does not* generally mean anywhere on the globe, but rather the **US of A, England or Canada (*AKA Big Farin*).** When a DJ tours *Big Farin,* he has indeed arrived. *(***Likkle Farin** is **Cayman** and other small islands.

Fassy: In the olden days, *fassy* was an **adjective** used to describe parts of the body that were covered with sores. **Example.** *Im foot fassy eeh!* In modern language however, *fassy* has become a **noun.** Sometimes it means a *male* *homosexual* and at other times it means a **traitor** or one who deliberately lets down or hurts his friends. You can determine the meaning from the context in which it is used.

Fi Mi Sinting: *(Sinting is optional for sometimes we simply say A fi mi etc.)* It means, *it's mine or I am the owner.* This is the singular. The plural of **Fi Mi** is **Fi Wi,** it is ours. When the property belongs to a third party, it becomes **Fi Dem**. *Fi Dem* is often used for both singular and plural as is *Fi Yu* which can be interchanged with *Fi Dem.*

Fi Real: "Yu a go Negril tinite? *Fi real?"* Are you really going to Negril tonight? **Fi Real** *means honestly or really......*usually used as an expressions of disbelief.

Flash : This means *to depart quickly.....leave the scene.* **Eg** *Mi a go flash now far it a get dark.* **Translation**. I have to leave now as it is getting late. However when **it** is added, (*flash it*) it means *to show off.* **Eg.** Look ow Spangler *a flash it* now dat im *bus out*.

Translation. Now that Spangler has become a big star, he is certainly showing off his wealth.

Flesh Dagger: *That which Mrs. Bobbit snipped ie. The male organ.*

Flex: *This describes a behaviour pattern* or *modus operandi.* **Example.** Mi nuh like ow yu a *flex*, yu nuh seet. **Translation.** I do not like how you are acting. However sometimes it is used to mean *to hang out* or *relax.* For example, one may say, "Mi a go *flex* wid mi fren dem till yu come, meaning, I am going to hang out with the guys until you get here.

Flex Corna: This is not where ordinary *"yute"* hang out but rather *blue light areas* where prostitutes "model" as they wait for customers to pick them up.

Fling Up; *Steal electricity.* Because they throw up electrical wires to connect to the pole of the official electrical provider, the term was coined.

Flip Up: *To act stupidly.*

Flop Mi Show: *Discourage me* or *be a disappointment to me.*

49

Follitrition: A sarcastic reference to a *politician*. A most appropriate description!

Forward: *An ovation given in the* **dancehall.** This is sometimes accompanied by gunfire. However, at *none dancehall* events, when a speaker at a function gets boring, a shout of "*forward*" may resound from the back of the room. This means *shut up* or *get lost* or it could very well mean "*come forward with something sensible.*" This new street language evolves so quickly that sometimes even I am confused*!*

Frass Out: *Messed up by drugs*. A sarcastic reference to the condition and behaviour of a *crack head, junki*e *or a person who has become addicted to some other mind altering substance*. Alternately, *Frazzle Out* is used.

Frenemy: *A hypocrite, enemy or backstabber*. (This is a combination of **friend** and **enemy**.) A synonym of *Diamond Sword*.

Frickshan: This means *turf war*. ...a usual explanation when violence breaks out in an area. However, sometimes it is more loosely used to refer to any type of *disturbance* or *disagreement,* even on an individual basis.

Frockles: *Another word for money, dunny, cash, dollaz...*whatever you want to call it.

Front En Lifta: A roots drink that is reputed to bail out i*mpotent or near impotent men.* Some men who cannot go on forever on their own, (a **Yardy** man's dream) also turn to this drink instead of the *ole time chiney brush*! In other words, it is an *aphrodisiac* made from local roots which neither **Viagra** nor **Cialis** can displace!

Fryas or Fryers: *These are low ranking gunmen who take orders from others* or are *sometimes mere gun bags*. **Example.** Mi nuh respec dem bwaay de far dem a *fryas*. **Translation.** I have no respect for those fellows for they are mere minions.

Full Undred: *Giving it all you've got, going all the way, total commitment* or *using maximum effort to complete a task.*

Fulla lyrics; *Glib.* One has to *be fulla lyrics* to be a successful **DJ.**

Fulla Stamina: *Energetic.* This phrase is commonly used in describing the ability of

reveler(s) to keep up with the fast,
pulsating pace of *dancehall* music.
Example: Di dawta *fulla stamina*
eeh? **Translation.** *I*sn't she just great
on the dance floor.

Fulla Vibes*: Rearing to go or feeling on top of the
world.*

Fya Bun Fi Yu or Fya Fi Yu: This is a phrase used to
condemn all and
sundry. **Example.** *Fya
bun fi* all battyman.
Translation. All gay
men should burn in
hell fire, or
alternately *down with
homosexuals.*

Fya Stick*: An unsophisticated name for a gun.*

Gaan Rub: Bleaching one's skin to lighten the complexion has now become a popular fad **a Yard**, as both men and women seem to want to reject their blackness. When people are said to *"gaan rub"* it means they have gone off to apply the bleach to their bodies in the hope of performing the longed for miracle....*becoming white!* I guess we could **blame Buju Banton** for his monster hit *Mi luv mi Browning* which seemed to have made black women feel terribly rejected.

Gal Inna Bungle*: Lots of girls.* This is generally used to describe two scenarios. Either by someone who is boasting that he has many girlfriends or by someone explaining to another that if he goes somewhere there will be no shortage of women to entertain him.

Gallis: *A Promiscuous man.* One who *has gal inna bungle.*

Get A Good Forward: This is the greatest thing that could happen to a DJ while on stage.

The term means to be *wildly applauded.* In certain circumstances, gun salutes and lighters are used to demonstrate just how highly the fans are rating the performance.

Get Bummy: *Let's have some fun* or *let it all hang out.* It also means *to become nervous* about something. In fact, it is a regular thing for the observation to be made that residents "*get bummy*" when certain notorious characters enter an area. You must pay close attention to the context in which this expression is used.

Get Jiggy; *Let's dance up a storm!* A typical suggestion that partners throw out to each other at the **dancehall.** Ocassionally, it is slackly used as a synonym of *get bummy*.

Get Wid Di Program: *Join in and have some fun.*

Giddy Giddy: The *dancehall* version of a *"Dumb blond".* All *dumb blond* jokes therefore apply to anyone so described. A synonym is **Giddy Head.**

Ghetto Corna: The *corner* on Mandela highway where *Beenie Man crashed his Hummer!* It is said that's where he got the *wickedest slam!* That was a joke going around about **Beenie Man** as before he crashed, he had made a monster hit saying the *wickedest slam* (sex) was to be found in the ghettos.

Ghetto Page: One of the most popular commodities a **Yard** is of course the cell phone, but unfortunately, many people who profile with one or even two or three cell phones, cannot afford the to buy phone cards. Being the relatives of *Anancy,* when a *Yardie* is broke, he uses the *ghetto page* to keep on chatting. This is done by calling someone and allowing the phone to **ring once.** As the number of the caller is displayed on the recipient's phone, if the call is returned, *the page* has been successful, that is a *Ghetto Page ie.* **Yardies** *samfie means of getting to chat on their phones all day,* *compliments of others' !*

Ghetto Slam: *Sex with a girl from the ghetto....*
supposedly the sweetest sex that an
uptown man could ever experience.
(according to the popular song)

Gi A Man Yam: The age old term for infidelity
is *gi a wan bun*. However it has
now become popular in **Trelawny** (a
parish on the north coast of **Jamaica**)
to change this term to *gi a man yam*.
This is because as **Trelawny** is the
yam capital a Yard so yam is far
more popular there than the lowly
bun!

Girlie Girlie: *A promiscuous man....a man who
has several girlfriends at the same time.*
Readers should note however
that such men are greatly admired in the
dancehall....only some of their
girlfriends complain! However there is a
theory that many young girls are more
easily attracted to **girlie girlie** men as
they think that rules out the possibility of
them being **gay,** a dangerous and
growing trend a **Yard!**

Go Pan a Works or Go Pan a Ends: *Make a move* or

go on a mission. (Rarely is it referring to going out to do anything above board.)

Go Low or Go Dung: *Oral sex when performed on a woman.* It is usually sung or spoken about negatively in the **dancehall** but everyone knows that *when most DJ's get off the stage or when the lights go out at home, it is a totally different ballgame!*

Goodas: *A lady with a perfect figure* or *a most desirable woman.* **Example:** Yu did know sey fi mi Joan a *goodas.* **Translation:** Did you know that my girl Joan has a perfect figure?

Gorgon: *"*Yu si di dread? Imma *gorgon* slapper roun ya know. **Translation.** That rastafarian gentleman is the biggest flirt in the area. *Gorgon* is an adjective used to describe *the best in the field.* So one can be *a gorgon banker, a gorgon D.J,* whatever. However when *Don Gorg*on is used, it becomes a noun.

Guh Easy: *Calm down.....don't get your blood pressure up!*

Gun Bag: *An inferior person in a gang whose only role is to transport weapons.* Those usually selected **are would be** gang members who are young and innocent looking *giving the impression that* he/she is beyond suspicion. However it is a well know practice for uniformed school children to be used as *gun bags.*

Gwany Gwany: *Pretentious, egotistical.*

Gyow: "Yu mussen mek dem deh man *gyow* yu so yu know." **Translation.** You should not allow yourself to be fooled by those scamps. When one **gyows,** he is either trying to make you look foolish or trying to con you in some way.

Gyow Ting: This simply means *foolishness.* A *gyow ting* yu a gwaan wid yu nuh seet. **Translation.** Please do not continue to bore me with your nonsense.

Hairy Bank: *A Prostitute*. **Example**: "Im always bruk far im carry im money go *hairy bank"*. **Translation**: He is always broke because he squanders all his money on prostitutes.

Hat It Up: (At It Up) Usually, a shout you hear at **dancehall** sessions meaning *'get jiggy"* or *"put some life into your performance man ,"*(usually accompanied by missiles thrown on to the stage or gun shots). If one hears a report that...*dem hat it up lass nite,* it would mean *"The vibes at the show were great last night.* On a more lethal plane, it could also mean *violence and mayhem erupted somewhere last night.* The context in which this expression is used has to be taken into consideration.

Head Nuh Good or **(Ead Nuh Good**): *Mad, crazy, loco.*

Hear Rumblings: *An omen. Some kind of warning.* **Example.** Danny nuh stap screw

far wen im go ome lass
nite im find sey im wifey gaan wid
im bredda, but a lang time mi did
hear di rumblings. **Translation.** I had
long heard the rumours about Danny's
wife but he only found out last night
when he went home and
discovered that she had left him
for his brother.

Hi Grade (I Grade): Ganja, marijuana, a
spliff...*the herb by whatever
name is just as sweet.* This is
definitely a staple in the **dancehall** and
for those who do not smoke, just
inhaling the fumes helps to get you in
the right mood.

Hian Bird (Ian bird): *An airplane.* **i.e.** a flying
machine made from metal.

Highly Bless: *A beautiful greeting* or *a reply to the
question "how are you?"*

Himbo; *A toyboy, one who is paid for sexual favours
by an older woman*

Hole (Ole)A Fresh : *Take a bath. Freshen up ones
self.* In the early days when
dancehall music was just

becoming popular, there
was a hit song with that title.

Hole (Ole) A Meds: *Relax, chill, meditate.* **Yardies** were sometime ago ranked in **an international happiness index** as the *third happiest people in the world.* While some scoffed at these findings, I am inclined to believe it since despite our huge problems, we have the ability to ***hole a meds***, (often with the help of the weed of wisdom) and that appears to be the key to our inexplicable happiness and carefree approach to everything!

Hole (Ole) A Wan-Two: Same as above.

Hole (Ole) Dat: *That's the truth* or *run with it.*

Hottie Hottie: *A sexy lady. A lady who is looking beautiful, well dressed and decked out in the finest garb,* although for **dancehall** sessions both women and men spare no expense to outdo each other. In the olden days, such a lady would be called **hot stuff.** However, only the women are dubbed **Hottie Hottie**. Unfortunately, some jealous women try to use the term disparagingly by sarcastically referring to their rivals as **hottie hotties**.

Hug Dat Up: *Too bad for you....tough luck etc.*
This is an expression used to let another know that he has to accept what the speaker has said or done for there is nothing he can do about it. In other words, *I man badda dan you.*

Hype Pan: *Show off or exaggerate.*

I an I or Iself: *The ital version of I or me.*

I An I Doan Wrap Up*: I am a no nonsense person or don't mess with me.*

Idren: *Friend, colleague. This is the ital version of bredren.*

Image: *An inconsequential person, an idiot, a shadow or a moron.* Very little hurts a **Yardie** more than to be called an ***image*** when he gets into a verbal dispute with another.

Im (H)Eead Gaan: *Gone off one's rocker, crazy, deranged.* This is used metaphorically in most instances however, to convey the impression that what the speaker is saying is outrageous. Alternately, the term **"*Im head nuh good"*** is used.

Informa: Only gay men are more hated in the **dance hall** than ***informas***. An ***informa*** is one who gives information to the police. As a result " ***infoma fi dead*** " has almost become mantra in the **dancehall.**

Inity: (Pronounced *I nity*) The *ital version* of **unity.**

Inna Mi Ackee: *I am feeling on top of the world.* The plural is *inna dem ackee*.

Irie: A great word used as a greeting or to describe *anything wonderful, pleasant or uplifting.*

Iself: *I, myself and m*e. Another version of *I an I.*

Ishh: "That's the latest style." It is sometimes used as an *adjective* however to describe *something trendy or new.*

It A Boom or It Deh Deh: *All is well or life is great.*

It A Di Lick: "*That's the latest style.*" Another version of *Ishh.* **Example;** Yu si di caar imma a drive since im buss out? *It a di lick* yu know. **Translation.** The car he has been driving since he became a star is the most expensive and popular vehicle among celebrities you know.

Ital: *Going natural in all spheres of life.* So some people, (especially *rastafarians*) eat only *ital food*…. that is, naturally grown food that have no additives. Of course, *ital sex* is sex without using any form of contraceptives or enhancers.

One who lives the *ital life* is called an *italist.*

Ital Jockey: Primarily, this is a man who indulges in *ital sex*. However another popular meaning is a man who performs well without the use of a *front en lifta, Cialil,* V*iagra* or any other enhancer.

Itis (Hitis): *A hit man* or *a contract killer.*

It Toosh: *An anticlimax...a wet squid* or *a flop.*

It Plug In Fi True: *It is perfect. Wasn't it wonderful*

Jah Lawn, Jamdung, or Jah Mek Ya: These are some of the popular names we use to refer to our dear little island of **Jamaica.**

Jockey: *The male partner during intercourse* Of course **dancehall** lyrics are full of suggestions as to how the jockey should ride.

Joe Grine: *The man who visits when the husband/ boyfriend is away. The other man , secret lover or person with* **whom bun is given.**

Jooker: *An ice pick.* However, this is not used to chip up ice, but rather *carried as a weapon.*

Juggle: *Organize.* Alternately, *go out to get money by any means.* **Example.** Bwaay, mi pickney dem haffi go a school so mi haffi go *juggle.* **Translation**. School has reopened, so I have to get some money to pay the kids' expenses.

Jucky Jucky: *Ones face when it is scarred and marred by acne.*

or bleaching. **Example**; Wat as way i*m face jucky jucky eeh!* **Translation;** Oh dear, look how his face has been damaged by the bleaching creams he has been using.

Jus Kool Man: *All is well, don't worry yourself, I have everything under control* etc. This term could be said to be the modern version of the *national motto* a **Yard,** *"No problem man."* However it is also used when someone is getting unnecessarily agitated, *jus kool man* then becomes a friendly order to *calm down* or *keep the temperature down.*

Kaya: *Another word for ganja* or *marijuana.* This is not a new word as it was popularized by **Bob Marley** some 30 years ago. However it remains in common usage in the *dancehall*.

Keep It Jiggy*: Greetings* or *all is well.*

Ketch Di Riddim or Ketch Di Vibes: *Another term for **Get Jiggy**.*

Ketch di Rake: *Interpret the signals that you are receiving* or *understand the hint you have been given.* We have become quite a gambling country so every dream and all occurrences are supposed to be giving us a hint about what numbers one needs to buy to hit the jackpot. One therefore has to develop the ability to *ketch di rake* to become a winner.

Kick Back: *Relax, let it all hang out.* **Example.** Mi nah go no wey tinite, mi jus a tan ome an *kick back.* **Translation.** I am busted so I am staying home to relax tonight.

Kin Teeth: *Act hypocritically.* This is really "skin

71

teeth" **ie.** show one's teeth or more specifically, *a false smile* while planning evil deeds against the person with whom you are smiling. Occasionally it is used as a synonym of **adamant. Ie.** *Smiling while refusing to budge.*

Kingfish; *A Toyota Corolla*. It is not unusual for us to give our own names to special cars. **Eg. Deportee, Skettel** etc. The **kingfish** is the type of vehicle that was used by the special *police squad* called **"kingfish"** hence in slang name was adopted to refer to all similar cars.

Kiss Mi Neck: This may not be a phrase which evolved during the **dancehall** era, but it is widely used there and every where else a **Yard**. This is simply an *expression of surprise or astonishment.*

Know Yu Self: An order to *be responsible and conscious of what one does and the possible repercussions*. This phrase is usually used when warning others to be careful.

Labba Labba: *One who talks incessantly is described as **labba labba** or **labba mout.***

Lasher*: A flerty flerty woman. A woman who sleeps around.* (Had I been in the business of inventing words for and phrases for use in the **dancehall,** I would call her a *Lashee*, but what can I tell you!)

Lay Lay: *Being unproductive, wasting time, hanging around, having nothing to contribute to the world etc.* Most of us a **Yard** are experts at *lay lay.*

Lef Or Rite? (*Literally left or right hand.*) You had better learn this phrase quickly as how you reply can determine you entire future! This question is asked only by *corrupt traffic cops.* If you reply **lef,** it means you are *willing to pay a bribe.* If you reply **rite**, it means you are refusing to pay so the cop *will be forced to write you a ticket!*

Lef a Ting Wid Mi Nuh? Could you give me

some money please. The
modern version of *beg yu
a money nuh.*

Let Off: *To give someone money for doing nothing.*
The *mantra* of a beggar. **Example.** *Let off* a
nanny pan mi nuh. **Translation.** Would
you be kind enough to give me $500 please?
This term is also used when one is on a bus
or route taxi and is requesting that it stops.
The shout *Let off*" or *"One Stop Driva"*
applies. Even when the bus has a bell or
other type of signaling device, most of us
Yardies prefer to yell at the driver.

Level: A friendly greeting or an expression of
agreement. **Example.** *Level* sista.
Translation. I totally agree with your point of
view or Hi Joan. Another meaning is *be totally
honest with me*. The context in which it is
used is therefore important.

Licky Licky: *Easily bought* or *a person who wants
everything (*without working for it*)*. A
person so described cannot be depended
on as his only loyalty *is to money* and
whoever plays the highest price has him
until a higher offer is made. Of course
this is a term that a lot of men a *Yard*

like to use to describe women but it applies to either sex.

Lik Out: *To condemn or criticize.*

Lik Shat: A phrase used in the *dancehall* to indicate that the artist who is performing should be wildly applauded. Often the applause takes the form of gun salutes, thus the term *lick shat.*

Lite A Man: *Kill someone.* (Literally!)

Livication: This is the **rasta** version of "*dedication*". As most **rastas** say they do not defend *dead things*, the word *dedication* has been elevated to *livication.*

Livity: *This is how a positive* and *holistic lifestyle is described.*

Lock Dung: *Draw down an immense crowd.* Draw such a large crowd that the area is jam packed, **ie.** *locked down.* When **dancehall** sessions are held and this happens, the artists are said to have *locked dung di area.*

Low Di Yute: *An order to leave someone alone.*

Lyrically Active: The ability to think up **dancehall**

lyrics *rapidly and spontaneously.*
This is a critical skill which must be
developed if one hopes to become a
successful *DJ.*

Lyrically Dead*: The very opposite of **Lyrically**
Active. This is what washed up
DJ's usually are.

Maama Man: *A homosexual man*. **Example**. Gwaay, mi nuh chat to *maama man*. **Translation**. Kindly leave me alone as I do not associate with homosexuals. A more moderate description of a *maama man* is one whom does tasks which were traditionally considered **woman's work**. Eg. Combing the children's hair!

Mampy: *An extremely obese woman*.

Man Nah Tek Nuh Dis: *No one would ever dare to disrespect me*. Expressions such as these are often used as a warning to those who are not well armed.

Mantel or **Montel**: *A village ram. A male skettel.*

Mash Up Di Place: An outstanding performance. When *a DJ/performer* is being wildly applauded, it is because he has pleased the *massives* ie. *mash up di place*.

Massive: Originally, *massive* referred to members of a gang. However the term is more widely used to refer to *any cohesive group* whether they operate for good or for evil. Another term for *massive* is *crew*. *Massive* most likely evolved from *masses* which was a popular word *in the political arena* in the70's.

Matey: (Sometimes spelt *matie*) This means *the other woman...the outside girlfriend* or *the female Joe Grine.*

Med Wid; *Chill out with friends.*

Mek A Duppy: *Kill someone.*

Mek Di Place Bummy: Another version of *mash up di place.*

Mek Mi Yey Zoom: This is a lovely expression. It means that something is said or done that is so *out of the ordinary* that it made one's eyes *pop out* in disbelief. In other words, " *I am flabbergasted.* "

Mek Ya. *Made in Ja (Jamaica).*

Mi A King Fram Creation: "*I am a true rastafari.*" A

79

Yard, there are many persons who wear *dreadlocks, smoke spliffs a*nd display other outward trappings to give the impression that they are *rastas* when they are nothing but imposters. When one says *Mi a king fram creation* he is trying to draw a line between the *true rasta* and *the imposters.*

Mi A Pree Yu: *Wow you look absolutely beautiful! I am admiring you.*

Mi Bisniss or Mi Tool: *My gun (or any other type of weapon.)*

Mi Check Fi Yu: *I love you dearly. Mi check fi im. I love him dearly etc etc.*

Mi Dawta: This is the very loving expression that a romantic *Yardie* man uses to refer to *his wife or favouritie girlfriend.*

Mi Doops: *A term of endearment like darling .* In the olden days it was *mi boonoonos.* It is occasionally used to address someone *who is loved or respected.*

Mi Links: *A friend. Someone who looks out for your*

best interest.

Mi Luv Yu More Dan Cook Food: It is pretty well accepted throughout the world that the way to a man's heart is through his stomach. A *Yard* however, it is a lovely hot **home-cooked meal** that seals it. So when a man declares *Mi luv yu more dan cook food,* he is saying *that he would basically give his life for you. That, my friends,* coming from any **Yard** man is true love!

Mi Nuh Ben Dung Fi No Man or **Mi Nah Duck***: I refuse to* or *would never consider having oral sex.*

Mi Nuh Penetrate Dat: *I do not agree with that* or sarcastically, *I am not impressed.*

Mi Nuh Penetrate Im: *I cannot stand that person (male or female)* or *I disapprove of his behaviour.*

Mi Nuh Response: *It is not my problem. Tough luck.*

Mi Pree: *My friend. A synonym of mi links.*

Miss Lipton: Another of the many terms used for a *male homosexual.*

Mi Wi Link Yu. I will be getting in touch with you.

Mix Up An Blenda: *Confusion caused by the rumour mill at its best. He says, she says, they say,* so many versions of a story going around that it leads to nothing but total confusion.

Monkey Lotion: *Acid when it is used as a weapon.* It is usually the preferred weapon of jealous women. **Example.** Lef mi man far mi nuh *skin up* fi *monkey lotion* ooman. **Translation.** Be careful how

you *come on* to my boyfriend as
I have no compunction about
throwing acid on women who
try to disrupt my home life.

More Dan Proportion: This is how a
voluptuous woman is
described..... her proportions
are better that everyone else's.

More Time: *See you later.*

More Nerve Dan A Bad Teet: *Literally this means*
"More nerve than a bad
tooth." Now, those of
us who have had a
tooth ache which feels
like millions of nerves
have been exposed,
can appreciate the
depth of this
expression. So when
we say a **Yard** that
someone has more
nerve dan a bad
teet, we are really
saying that the person
is the *epitome of*
brazenness or just

83

extremely impudent.

Move Im Up*:* Another of the dozens of terms meaning to *kill someone*. A synonym of *mek a duppy, nyam im food etc.*

Movements: *Goodbye, see you later, I'm off* etc.

Mr. Faggoty: Another term for a *male homosexual.* (A variation of the popular English word "faggot').

Mr. Mention: *A man who likes to profile and show off. A vain man.* In the olden days, the term for a vain man was *pretty boy Floyd* .

Mumma Mongrel: *A promiscuous woman.* A synonym of *Lasher, Skettel, Ole Bike Flerty- Flerty, Bomshell* etc. You will note how many words and phrases are coined in the *Dancehall* to describe such women while only one or two are invented describe men who *sleep around.* What does this tell you?

Mumsy: *A polite term* used by young people when

they greet women who are older than they are.

My Yute: This is sometimes a *greeting* simply meaning *"hello"* or it can be used as the pronoun *You.* Literally however it means, *young man*. **Example.** *My yute*, bring da nanny cum gimmi nuh. **Translation**. Young man, please pass me that $500 note.

Now A Days Yout: Most times this is used to refer to ***the younger generation*** but it is sometimes used to refer to *people in general.*

Nuff Lyrics: *Having the gift of gab.* Also where **DJ's** are concerned this refers to those who have the ability to ***toast*** (ie. Coin lyrics spontaneously.)

Nuff Niceness: An *all encompassing* very pleasant expression, sometimes a *greeting, a farewell* or sometimes simply ***"have a nice day*** or ***all is well".***

Nuff Rispec: Another pleasant phrase used *to bid friends farewell, to indicate that all is well* or *sometimes an expression indicating that one is in agreement with something said* or *done.*

Nuh: In the olden days (ie. Last month), ***nuh*** meant *don't* or *no.* **Eg.** Mi nuh waan nuh *ziggy,* mi waan a B*ob* M*arley.* **Translation.** Don't give me that little spliff. However, it now means ***no nonsense***. So if some **fryers** is about to do something silly, a simply ***nuh*** from the *Don* *stops him in his tracks..*

Nuh Hab Nuh Broutupsi or **Nuh Hab Nuh Behavia**:
An ill mannered or poorly brought up person is described using either of these phrases or *if one does or says something inappropriate*, it might just illicit that comment.

Nuh Jester: *To be dead serious* or *to have no compunction about being violent.* **Example.** My yout, *mi no jester* yu know, so jus *know yu self* an nuh mess wid mi. **Translation.** Please be careful how you approach me as I am a very serious person and hurting people comes naturally to me.

Nuh Kin Up: A synonym of *nuh jester* **Example.** Dat dey man *nuh kin up* far if yu tep pan im toe im shat yu. **Translation.** I would never get entangled with that man as he is too cold-blooded

Nuh Press Mi Button: *Do not annoy me.* It can also mean, *do not dare to try ordering* or *pushing me around.*

Nuh Seh Nutten: *Don't worry. Just remain cool.*

Nuh Wile Dem: *Let's surprise them or let them remain happy in their ignorance.* **Example.** Dem tink dem bad but *nuh wile dem*. **Translation.** They think they are invincible but we have a surprise for them.

Nutten Nah Gwaan: *Times are hard....life is difficult* .This is favourite reply of just about every *Yardie* (including the rich and famous) to the question "*How are you?*"

Nyam Im Food: *Murder someone* or *take by force something that belongs to another.*

Nyam Unda Di Sheet.: *Engage in oral sex.*

Nyammi Nyammi: *Greedy.* A synonym is *Wanga Gut.* **Example.** Mi cyaan tek out Joan again far shi too *nyammy nyammy*. **Translation.** I could never afford to date *Joan* again because every time we go out she wants to eat everything in sight.

Ole Bam: *The ex-girlfriend.* **Example**. Cho man, Dulcie a mi *ole bam* so shi can do weh shi waan. **Translation.** I don't care what Dulcie does as I am no longer in love with her.

Ole Bike: *A promiscuous woman, but one who is no longer desireable. A loose woman who has already played the entire circuit, ie has been ridden by each and every interested man!*

Ole Dawg: *A gun.* **Example**. Mi nuh go nuh wey widdout mi *ole dawg* yu know, far di man dem a road too wikkid.
Translation. It is so dangerous living in these times that I never leave home without my gun.

Ole Foot: *A lady who is over the hill and cannot find a male mate.* The modern phrase for an **old maid.**

Ole Fya Tick: A synonym of *ole bam.*

Ole Pazart: *Another name for a boopsie...a female parasite.*

Ole Scaliba: *A fearless gunman.* **Example.** Dem dey man no fraid a Babylon or no man far dem a *ole scaliba.* **Translation.** Those men are not afraid of the police or anyone else because they are well armed and fearless.

Ole Tight: *Wait, hang on, do not change what you are doing* etc. This is really the street version of *"stay put."* It should actually be **"hold tight"** but you know how we like to treat our "*h*"

One Burna: *A man who keeps only **one woman at a time**. .....a faithful man*! Of course, this is a most unusual member of *the male species* a *Yard.* This phrase is therefore usually used (by men of course) as an *insult* or to *show disdain.*

Oreo Man: *A black man who only dates brownings*. Oreo is of course a cookie that is dark outside but white inside, hence one who is ashamed of being black is also an *oreo man.* The old time version of this phrase is *roast breadfruit*.

Original Mobster or Original Stepper:
> *A gunman...a criminal.*

Out An Bad: An adjective meaning *fearless*.

Overlap or Eberyting Lock: *Everything is taken care of* or *all the arrangements have been made.* This is usually used in terms of arrangements to be made for some upcoming event.

Overstan: *Understand.* The theory behind this is that if you have knowledge, you are *over the hurdle* not *under* as *English* dictionaries would have you believe. A very intelligent deduction indeed!

Pack Up and Park: *Leave the stage*. An expression used at *Dance Hall* sessions to indicate that the audience is unimpressed with the performance. **Example**. Ay bwaay, yu l*yrically dead* so *jus pack up an par*k. **Translation. Boo!**

Page Im: *Murder someone*. The theory being that the murder will be reported in **the** *pages* of the newspaper. Gone on the days when there was a less lethal meaning **ie.** A form of c*ommunication..* **Eg.** *Page im...give him a call, try and find him etc.*

Pan Handle: *A stupid woman*.

Par: *Friend*, (spar)

Par Wid: *Get together with friends to party and have fun*. **Example.** Mi a go *par* wid mi bredren dem far the road black and mi caan go a work. **Translation.** I am going to go out and enjoy myself with my friends as there is a demonstration and the roads are blocked, so I can't go to work

Passa Passa: *Mix up, confusion or contention.*
> **Example.** Mi gaan far mi nuh inna
> nuh *passa passa* wid har.
> **Translation.** Let me get out of here as
> I hate contention. The term was
> however adopted for a **dance session**
> held every Wednesday night in
> Western Kingston and it became so
> successful that it got worldwide
> exposure.

Paro: *A drunkard*

Pazart: *A woman who depends on men for her*
> *financial existence. A female parasite.*
> *Another name for a Boopsie.*

Peanut: *An inadequate male organ. A very small*
> *penis. The opposite of Anaconda.*

Peeps. *One's family or close friends. Also an*
> *endearing term for one's children.* **Mi peeps** is
> now very widely used to refer **to all ones**
> **loved ones.**

Penetrate: *Meditate, understand.* An alternate
> meaning is to *visit or attend......visit a*
> *session or go out to a dance.*

Permanent Head Damage: *This is what the*

treated. (In other words not just *poop inna.*) **Ray Ray goods** *are cleaned, washed, painted etc for resale.* And where are these goods sold? You guessed it. At **the Ray Ray Market** of course! In *big farin*, these outlets are known as **Thrift Stores.**

Ray Tay: *This and that, odds and ends.*

Ready Fi Wine: *Feeling horny.*

Religwrong: *The religious denomination or philosophy with which the speaker disagrees.*

Ride Bare Back: *When a man has sex without using a condom he is said to ride bare back.* One aspect of *ital sex.* This is a practice engaged in, in the main, by men and women *who are interested in getting AIDS!*

Rinse Gun Inna Man Face: *To intimidate or threaten someone with a gun.*

Rispeck, Raspeck Or Rispeck Due: A general term meaning *I agree with you, I salute you, I respect you* or *have a good*

Example. Nuh press mi button far mi nuh hab patience wid eediat.

Pretty Lakka Money: *Absolutely beautiful*. ie. ***as pretty as money!***

Profile: This is a verb meaning *to show off or to model*. (be well decked out.) **Example.** Wen dem dey gal go a dance a pure profile dem a profile. **Translation.** When those young ladies go out to party they are perfectly decked out. In the olden days, they said *dressed to kill*.

Programme: *Check out, assess, observe keenly.*

Pum Pum Possee: *Ladies of the night, loose women.*

Pum Pum Printer: *A pair of tights which when worn by a woman leaves nothing to the imagination.*

Punnani: *A slack reference to a lady's vagina.* Originally the colloquial term was *pum pum,* and whereas this is still used, *punnani* is the more popular word used these days.

Rail and Drap: *Rough sex.*

Rail Up: *Be energetic like **Elephant Man** on the dance floor.* In the olden days, they said *fling foot*. It can also be used in reference to when one *loses his/her temper.*

Ram Di Place: *Draw a magnificent crowd.* Same as **sell aff.** **Example**. Dem dey bwaay a gwaan wid foolishness. Yu si wen mi put on a session? A nuff money mi mek yu know, far mi get DJ dat *can ram di place*. **Translation.** What a financial disaster for the promoter. That would never happen to me as when I put on a session I get top of the line performers who attract a large crowd.

Raspec: This is the *ital* version of *respect.*

Ray Ray: *"And so on and so forth"*. This was the original meaning and the phrase is still used in this context at times. However it has also evolved to mean *second hand goods,* but second hand goods specially treated. (In other words not just *poop inna.*) **Ray Ray goods** *are cleaned, washed, painted etc for resale.* And where are these goods sold? You guessed it. At **the Ray Ray Market** of course! In *big farin*, these outlets are known as **Thrift Stores.**

Ray Tay: *This and that, odds and ends.*

Ready Fi Wine: *Feeling horny.*

Religwrong: *The religious denomination or philosophy with which the speaker disagrees.*

Ride Bare Back: *When a man has sex without using a condom he is said to ride bare back.* One aspect of *ital sex.* This is a practice engaged in, in the main, by men and women *who are interested in getting AIDS!*

Rinse Gun Inna Man Face: *To intimidate or threaten someone with a gun.*

Rispeck, Raspeck Or Rispeck Due: A general term meaning *I agree with you, I salute you, I respect you* or *have a good*

day, goodbye, etc….anything pleasant.

Risto: *An uptown person or a person of means.* (An aristocrat.)

Roach Killa: Another name for *shoes*. I guess this arose because so many persons use their shoes *to kill the pesky cockroach*. Our **DJ's** are so creative.

Rope Een: *Come here please, join us (me), lets go out and have fun etc.*

Rrrrr: The new hip way of saying *hello*. Don't try it if you do not know how to roll your *r's*. I suspect that whoever started this wanted to say something else, (*which is also often used as a greeting*) but a policeman was in hearing distance!

Run A Boat: This is **not** a new phrase and it was **not** invented in the *dancehall*. However it remains such a popular concept a *Yard* that it has to be included in this publication. You **run a boat** when a group of persons get together and buy the ingredients to cook a meal *for all* to partake in. ie. *community cooking*. It is sometimes

101

done **because** individually, no one
member of the group has enough funds
to finance a proper meal and at other
times, just as a means of *partying or
socializing*. Whatever the motivation,
r*unning a boat* is a most enjoyable
practice and regular pastime a **Yard**
although uptown people try to sanitize
it by saying they are having a *basket
party*.

Run Di Road: *To be in control/in charge of an
area.* **Example**. Yu si da simple
looking yout dey. Well no tek im
so far a im run di road.
Translation. That young man
appears to be harmless but do not take
any chances with him for he is in control
of the entire area.

Run Wid It: *Accept it for what it is. That's how it
has to be.*

Runnings: *A synonym of bandoolo.*

Rupshan: *Confusion, any type of disturbance.*

Saaf It Out: *Ignore something, not bother one's self.*

Saafas: *An ineffective person. One who is easily manipulated or bossed around.*

Saaaf Han(An) Man: *A mean man. One who gives no financial support to his family but is not against exploiting his mate financially.*

Same Ole Same Ole: *The more things change the more they remain the same.*

Sample: *A simpleton, moron or idiot.*

Satan Plan: *Any wicked act.*

Scallawa: *A criminal or a worthless person.*

Schoolas: *Students. Children who wear uniform.* (This term is usually used to describe pre-teens).

Screechie: *To sneak around, move stealthily, to go underground.* **Example**. Wen dem dey man start **screechie** yu know sey some friction a gwaan. **Translation.** Whenever

103

you see certain persons acting mysteriously you know some form of disturbance is at hand.

Screw: *To make up one's face in anger or disgust.*

Screw Face: *A wicked or evil looking person.*

Seaga Face, Pattison Bady: *How the idiots who bleach their faces to look fair skinned are sometimes scornfully described.* When they bleach, the body (arms and neck especially) remain dark while the face gets fair, so since former prime minister *Seaga* is white and former prime minister *Patterson* black, a creative **DJ** came up with the expression.

Seen; This has multiple meanings such as *all is well, goodbye, I understand you, hello etc.*

Seen Dads Or Seen Mumsy: This is another variation of *seen* . When *seen* is used with these nouns *it is a polite form of greeting* used by the younger generation to those older than they are to demonstrate that they respect their elders.

Seh Bout: *Is that so? Or it might simply mean "I agree with you."*

Selfist: *One who has sex by himself/herself. One who loves to masturbate.* In the olden days male comics would say, I am enjoying myself with **Sarah Palmer** *and her five girls.*

Sen Man A Shap: *To treat another with disrespect.* This term evolved from the world of the gangs, where those young men who are **not** considered hardened or cold blooded enough, are used as mere messengers or to transport weapons. It is somewhat of a synonym of *gun bag.*

Sell Aff; *An overwhelming success.* It is a distortion of **sold out.**

Set A Way: *It is predestined. That's life.*

Shack Out: *Relax, let it all hang out.*

Shi Ancuff Im: Men who are categorized as such are not usually respected in the eyes of their peers. For *shi ancuff im* means the man in question is under

the total control of his girlfriend/
wife and therefore cannot move a
muscle or spend a dollar without her
permission. In other words, she has
*him in handcuffs.....he can do nothing
without her permission.*

Shizzle: Ask *Elephant Man*. I have not been able to
find anyone who can give a definite
translation of this creation of his. Anyway he
uses to it in a pleasant manner every time so
who cares what it really means?

Shock Out: *Well dressed, dressed to kill.* (Not
literally of course.

Shotta: Another name for a *gunman.*

Sick Inna Im Ead: *Crazy, loco, ridiculous.* The
normal reaction to a stupid
suggestion *is im sick inna im ead.*

Siddung Pan It: This is advice that is usually given
to young girls. It means that one
should not give in to the wiles of a
particular gentleman and have sex
with him. In other words, abstain,
*do not allow yourself to be seduced
by smooth talking men.* In the olden

days mothers and grandmothers would
urge their young girls *to keep their
legs crossed*! (Be coy about sex)

Siddung Pan Man Eyelash: To be *financially
dependant on a man.*
Example. Look pan Dulcie
ow shi a suffa. Is cause shi
always a siddung pan man
eyelash an as dem blink shi
drop off.
Translation. Poor Dulcie is
such a woeful sight. It is
because has spent her entire
life depending on men instead
of trying to support herself
why she is now in dire straits
why she is totally broke now
that he has left her.

Site Di Rake: *To catch on.* (To some scheme or
plan to fool someone or con them in
some way.)

Skettel: This word tends to evolve on a regular basis.
It was originally coined to describe a
cheap woman, especially one that had
become *so used up* that no man wants to be
seen with her. Then it was widened to

describe *cheap things in general*. So for example you would hear about *skettel drinks, skettel clothes etc.* Now, we even have a car called *skettel.* This is the ubiquitous *white station wagon* which is often used as a taxi and which almost always is described as the vehicle *seen leaving a crime scene*. This vehicle is called a *skettel* as it is *so cheap* that anyone can buy it hence it has become extremely common.

Skin Up: *To have no compunction about committing an evil act*. **Example.** Mi nuh *skin up* fi rinse gun inna bwaay face, yu nuh seet! **Translation.** I have absolutely no compunction about shooting people.

Slam: Another word *for sexual intercourse*. You will note that sex is a permanent hang up in the d*ancehall*.

Slap The Cat: *Another uncouth reference to sexual intercourse. (That's three in a row. Wow!)*

Slapper: *One who sleeps around....a flirt.*

Slap It: A most derogatory term *for a man having*

sexual intercourse with a woman.
(The woman is the *it!*).

Small Up Yuself: *Excuse me please*. This
expression is used when one
wants to pass another but the
space is inadequate. This chorus is
regularly heard in *minibuses and
route taxis.*

Smell Green: To *reek, have a strong body odour.*
Example. Mi nuh luv fi travel inna
skettel far di man dem *smell
green.* **Translation.** I hate to travel
in the cheap route taxis as the
passengers tend to have strong body
odours.

Sort Out: *Good sex.* The **Jamaican** male's solution to
every problem a woman has....**shi waan
sort out.**

Soun Clash: This is an exciting event where *sound
systems operators* try to outdo each
other. The evidence of who is winning
is expressed by the number and calibre
of *forwards* that each disc jockey
receives. However, when 'one simply
refers to a *Clash*, it is a *live
competition* between **DJ's** on stage.

109

The idea here is to see who can **spontaneously** deliver the **best lyrics** to **mash up** the show

Spangy Di Pants: *Extra tight pants.* One of the latest fads among many young boys. In other words, these pants are adjusted to fit like *spandex.* The term is usually associated with male homosexuals.

Spar: (n) *Friend, brethren.* **As a verb,** spar *means to have fun or to hang out with friends.* **Example.** Mi a go dung di road fi *spar* wid mi bredren dem. **Translation.** I am going to hang out with my friends for a while.

Spice: *A box. I don't mean the container, but rather a blow to the face.* This is a tribute to the *DJ Spice* who was recently boxed by a detractor after a session. So if someone promises you a *spice,* don't go thinking you are going to get a box of goodies, but rather a blow to remember!

Spliff: *A marijuana cigarette.* There are two popular sizes, the *Bob Marley* and the *Ziggy.*

Splurt: (Sometimes spelt *Splert*). *To run away, escape or simply to leave the scene quickly.*

110

Example. Si mi dawta a come. Mi
haffi *spurt* far mi did tell ar sey mi
gaan a wok. **Translation.** Oh my
goodness, here comes my girlfriend. I
have to get out of here immediately
because I had told her that I was going
off to work.

Star: *A general term used to address anyone.*
Example. Yow *star,* gimmi a nanny nuh?
Translation. Hello nice lady, can you give me
$500 please? This term can be used to address
anyone and in any tone...friendly, ominous or
whatever.

Status: *What a well endowed lady has....ie. a great
body.* **Example.** Mi nuh deal wid ooman who
nuh hab status. **Translation.** I only date
women with beautiful figures.

Step Off: *Die. A synonym of Drap aff.* This is
usually said with great sadness.

Step Up Time: *Time to move up in the world, get
rich ore improve one's lot by hook
or by crook.* When one succeeds it
is said that "*im step up inna
life.*"

Stepper: *An armed robber, a criminal, or gunman.*

Stoosh; *Conceited, full of ones self.* However, it is often used to **convey envy** in describing persons who are well dressed. **Eg.** Im stoosh yu si. **Translation;** He dresses well but I would never let him know that I thought so!

Strait Up: *That's how it is, honestly, that's the truth etc.* Sometimes the "up" is dropped and one simply says *strait*. It means the same thing.

Strika: *A playboy, a girlie girlie man.* Mr. *luvva luvva* a la **Shaggy.**

Strong Back: *An aphrodisiac made from local roots.* There is very little that *Yardie* men like to boast about more than their sexual prowess and they have no qualms about taking whatever improve their they can get top performance. So most men a *Yard* will unashamedly tell you that have a special supplier/manufacturer of a *miracle drink (read strong back)* which they swear makes them the greatest *strikers* on earth!

Struggle: *Dance.* This is **not** the name of a dance however, but rather it is a **verb** meaning *to dance.* **Example.** Yow gal, gimmi a

> ***struggle*** pan di bady nuh?
> **Translation.** Will you dance with me
> please?

Suck Off Two Bills: *Get money from someone*
without working for it. ***Con***
someone out of money.

Superintendent: *The official woman, the wife or*
main girlfriend. (***The one who***
gives the orders!)

Suss: *Rumour, scandal.*

T

Tadpole: *A young man who is being paid for his sexual favours by an older woman. Ie.* A man who is being kept by an older woman. A synonym of ***himbo*** or ***toyboy.***

Tap A Di Tap*: A well respected person. One who is outstanding in some respect.*

Tekker: *A Thief or robber.*

Tek A Chill Pill Nuh: *Relax, or calm down.* Usually it is a suggestion made to people who are agitating themselves unnecessarily.

Tek Charge: *Take control of a situation and bring about some semblance of order.* It is however often used in reference to ***male/female relationships.*** When it is, it means the man has won over a woman and now controls her life.

Tek Libety Wid: *Disrespect someone, be rude to another.*

Tekeisha: *A greedy woman, an exploiter.* All she is interested in a man for is his money to *tek, tek , tek, tek*, even if she just met him.

Ten Toe Turbo: *Walking barefooted.* (Not because of style but finances.) **Example.** A jus di odda day im dey pan *ten toe turbo*, now koo pan im a dribe crissas. **Translation.** Only recently he was walking barefooted, now look at the beautiful car that he is driving!

Tings A Gwaan: Any kind of activity but most often *violence* resulting from some kind of friction. **Example.** *Tings a gwaan* between Spangler and Dudus cause Spangler tief Dudus ooman. **Translation.** Spangler and Dudus are at war because Dudus dated has girlfriend. When *Fi Yu , Fi Mi* or *Fi Dem* is added, the meaning is less lethal as it simply means that *one is moving up in life*. **For example**, if one has a look of prosperity eg. *Cargo Chain, BMW* etc. you might very well say "*wait tings a gwaan fi Joan*." This simply means that Joan is showing signs that her fortunes have improved.

Tishan: The street slang for *politician.* It is not used in a respectful manner.

Toast: *The ability to coin lyrics on stage spontaneously* (like *Ninja Man*) or in general to speak glibly. So when a man is propositioning a woman, he is often said to be t*oasting* her.

Traila Load A Gal: *Numerous women as in a harem. What promiscuous men claim they have.* It is also considered a mark of success in the *dancehall,* for the more baby mothers that a **DJ** can boast about, the more he is revered. **Wayne Marshall**, take a bow for courageously standing up against the popular *"cultra"* and promoting responsible family life.

Trash An Ready: *Beautifully decked out.* (Dressed to kill). How every true blooded *dance hall adherent* strives to look when going out on the town.

Trus Mi: *I would never lie to you. This is gospel, I swear etc*. **Never** trust anyone who punctuates every sentence with the phrase *trus mi.*

Tuff: *Wonderful, great or nice.*

Tugs: This was originally a synonym of *shotta* (meaning a gunman.) It has however evolved to mean f*riend* or *spar* when preceded by **mi.**

Twenty Eight: *A machete.* (The poor man's "38" ie. Gun.) **Example**. Dem bwaay jus come fram country so dem nuh know sey *twenty eight* nuh run tings ya. **Translation.** Being new to the city, those young men do not know that mobsters use guns not machete.

Twin Cam: *A man who has sex with both men and women. An ACDC man.*

Unda Mi Nose: *The nerve. The epitome of shamelessness.* When someone does something disgusting or controversial **openly.**
Example. Imagine mi owna sista Doreen a check mi man *unda mi nose.* **Translation.** Imagine Doreen, my own sister, has been making passes at my boyfriend front of me. To emphasise how disgusting the act is, one could add *"Shi hab more nerve dan a bad teet"*

Unda Mi Sensi*: Feeling irie.* Since *sensi* (which is only grown a *Yard,*) is the best quality ganja in the world, the term originally meant *feeling high after having smoked it.* The term has however evolved to simply mean *feeling high.*(after having used any product, natural or chemical.)

Visa: *Hard to get, or scarce*. (Like a US visa).**Example.** Ow mi caan si yu. Yu come in lakka *visa*.**Translation.** How is it that I rarely see you around anymore? Recently, a number of **DJ's** lost their US visas and it was like the end of the world to them.

Vitamin S: *Sex*. **Example.** A wha mek yu so miserable. A *vitamin S* yu waan? **Translation.** Is it because you have not had sex for a long time why you are so cranky.

Waa Uunu Dey Pan: A very general question meaning *what's happening, what are you up to, do you have anything interesting on the agenda* etc. or even *how are you?*

Wagonist; *One who likes to be identified with the success of others and popular causes although having no true conviction....a hypocrite.* The **Yard** version of one who likes to jump on the band wagon.

Wanga Gut: *A greedy person.* **Example.** Bwaay mi si waan buffilous dawta and tek ar go show, but di gal a waan wanga gut an woudda nyam out mi packet.
Translation. I met this beautiful young lady and invited her to the movies, but she wanted to eat everything in sight and nearly bankrupted me.

Wash Gun Inna Bwaay Blood: *Shoot someone at close range.*

Wat A Go Dung or Wat a go dung: *What's happening? Is there any action afoot, are you doing anything today* etc?

Welding Torch: A synonym of *Anaconda*. In other words, a *large penis*. (What every *Yardie* man claims to have!)

Well Conscious: *On the ball, aware of what is happening, intelligent* etc.

Well Cole: *Extremely wicked, vicious, dawg hearted.*

Western Union: Modern *Yardies* have no problem incorporating the names of private establishments into their vocabulary. *Western Union* is synonymous with money, so as many *Yardies* here depend on that organization to bring their monthly income. So would you believe that now *Western Union* is another term for a *Boops?*

Wheel an Come Again: *Try once more, come with a better story, or I remain unconvinced.*

This is generally used as an expression of disbelief. **Example.** Imagine di bwaay tell mi sey im nuh married wen every day wi si im a profile wid ooman. Mi haffi tell im fi *wheel an come again.* **Translation.** This very brazen young man had the nerve to tell me he wasn't married although we all know otherwise. I had to tell him to come with a better story than that.

Wi Flex Good: *We get on well together....we understand each other.* **Example.** Mi an mi dawta a go rung fi five ear now far *wi flex good.* **Translation:** I have been going steady with my girlfriend for five years and we will stay together for many years to come as we understand each other.

Wi Hab Di Ting Lack: (*Eberyting Lock Up).* *We are in control. Don't worry.* This is usually the reply given when one has been given a task and later asked how things are proceeding. The modern version of *"No problem."*

Wi Rule: (or **A wi rule** or **A mi rule**: *I/we are in charge here or I/we are the boss.*

Wicked: *Great, wonderful.*

Woom Twista: *A very large penis.* A synonym of ***Anaconda.***

Word: *"I agree with you."* **Example.** Di show di odda nite did nice eeh? Reply. *Word.* **Translation.** Wasn't it a fabulous show the other night? Reply. Oh yes, it most certainly was!

Worlian: *A materialistic or ungodly person . One to whom money is the be all and end all.*

Wow: *Yardies* have the unique ability of taking the most traditional word and turning it on its head. *Word* above is one such an example. So is *Wow,* that innocuous word which has for generations been simply an expression of astonishment. Well that was in the olden day, for today's street lingo has determined that *wow* now means *all is well* or *fine thank you*. It is now in common usage as the reply to the question *"How are you?*

Yard: *Jamaica, Jamdown, home sweet home.* .**ie**. The greatest place on earth.

Yardie: *Originally, a Jamaican who lived (or operated) overseas however it is more generally used to describe anyone who was born "a Yard" or maybe who was born abroad, but has adopted our Yardness.*

Yow: *Hello, or an equivalent friendly greeting.*

Yu A Get Bun: *Your wife/husband is being unfaithful to you... has someone else on the side!*

Yu Corna Dark: *You are in serious trouble or you are unlucky.* **Example.** Bwaay *yu corna dark* far as yu go inna di bank di wrecker cum tek wey yu cyaar. **Translation.** Today is just not your day for as soon as you went into the bank the wrecker came along and towed away your vehicle.

Yu Criss: *You are perfectly correct or don't worry.*

Yu Dun Know: *You have to agree or you have to accept what is being said or done.* **Example.** From di babylan sey a so a so. *Yu dun know.* **Translation.** When the police give you an order you just have to do what as you are told or else.

Yu Nuh Ready: *Try again or insultingly, you are stupid, incompetent* etc.

Yu Nuh Seet ,Yu Seet or Yu Si Mi: *That's so obvious, or do you understand?*

Yu Penetrate Dat: *Do you understand or do you agree?* (same as above)

Yu Salt : *You are so bad lucked, I am so sorry for you or things are just not going your way. Mi Salt* is used when the person speaking *is the one* experiencing the bad luck. **Example.** Bwaay, *mi salt* far fi di hole year mi nuh sell wan house. **Translation.** I think I am going to get out of this business because I have not sold a house for the entire year!

Yu Too Nuff: *You are full of it.* What you say to a conceited person.

Yush: *Wonderful or well done.* Also another version

of *hi or how are you.*

Yute An Yute: *Everyone, all and sundry or no one in particular.* **Example.** Yu si ow Frenchie a walk street since im tun coke head? All him nebba know sey *yute an yute* nuh fi touch dem dey tings? **Translation**. Look how Frenchie is now living on the streets. Didn't he know that cocaine would have made him mad.

Zeen: Another pronunciation of *seen,* with its multiple meanings such as *all is well, goodbye, I understand you, hello etc.*

Ziggy: *A small spliff* (marijuana cigarette). ***Bob Marley*** has a famous poster with him smoking a very large spliff hence the large spliff is called the ***Bob Marley*** and the smaller size has been named after his young, famous son ***Ziggy.*** **Example.** Hey bass, mi nuh hab nuh money tidday so gimmi a *ziggy* nuh. **Translation.** As I am short of funds I can only afford to buy a small spliff today, so please oblige.

EXTRA, EXTRA, READ ALL ABOUT IT HERE!

No man bizness…..that is the mantra of some of our esteemed *dancehall stars* who are extremely *homophobic.* So some have now adopted the trend of changing every name containing the word *man* in it to *gal* when performing.

So *Man*chester has now become *Gyal*chester. *Man*deville has become *Gyal*deville and even poor little **Grand Cayman** has become **Grand Caygyal!**

Aren't you happy you bought as copy of **the 6th Edition of the Original Dancehall Dictionary**, for without it you would have been totally confused when trying to interpret what is being said by the youngsters a **Yard!**

Walk good.

Joan

ABOUT THE AUTHOR

Joan Williams, who could loosely be described as a returning resident, is a qualified *Real Estate Dealer*. She is also a well known *free lance journalist*. Over the years Mrs. Williams has written columns for the *Gleaner*, *Star*, *Observer* as well as several other newspapers and magazines which have long since ceased publication. She continues to write an occasional column for the Miami based *Caribbean Today* and sits in when necessary as the *alternate host* of the popular talk show, *Perkins on Line*.

Mrs. Williams, founder of *Yard Publications* has authored several books including six *Back A Yard* publications (Back A Yard was an annual satirical review of Jamaican life and politics) and *Tour Jamaica*. For the kids, she published, *The Original Jamaican Colouring Book, Count and Colour, Colour and Learn* and *Draw and Colour*, all designed to help kids learn about and appreciate the beauty of Jamaica.

She can be contacted at @gratestj@gmail.com. Also, you can visit her at; http://joan-myviews.blogspot.com/